T0198687

LORD, TEACH ME HOW

Building Your Faith by Prayer and God's Word

ELIZABETH BAXTER

WestBow Press books may be ordered through booksellers or by contacting:

WestBow Press
A Division of Thomas Nelson & Zondervan
1663 Liberty Drive
Bloomington, IN 47403
www.westbowpress.com
844-714-3454

Author Photo Credit: Morgan Kitchen Freelance Photographer and Creator
Website: www.morgankitchen.com
Instagram: @morgan.xyz

Good News Translation:
Scripture quotations marked (GNT) are from the Good News Translation in Today's English Version-Second Edition Copyright © 1992 by American Bible Society. Used by Permission.

ISBN: 978-1-6642-6869-2 (sc)
ISBN: 978-1-6642-6870-8 (e)

Print information available on the last page.

WestBow Press rev. date: 07/14/2022

WESTBOW
PRESS®
A DIVISION OF THOMAS NELSON
& ZONDERVAN

LORD,
TEACH
ME HOW

LORD, TEACH ME HOW:

Building Your Faith by Prayer and God's Word

ELIZABETH BAXTER

With loving memories of my dad, Headley
praying with me as a child.
Dedicated to my daughter, Annelize.

Lord, teach me to be brave.
No fear, be strong, and not to cave.
In victory, my hands to wave.
Lord, help me to be brave.
Psalm 144:1; Isaiah 28:26

ACKNOWLEDGMENTS

I would like to acknowledge my parents for setting an atmosphere of prayer in our home, especially my mother. For as long as I can remember, prayer has been an integral part of our family life. Growing up in the 1980s, I remember my mother, along with her prayer warrior partners, prayed several times a day using the newly introduced conference call feature on our phone. Hearing my mother pray as I got ready for school laid the foundation for this book. I desired my own prayer life with God, but I did not know how. My prayer life was short, quick, and to the point, including grace before eating. Maybe two minutes at most, or five minutes when I was entreating God for a favor. Basically, I didn't pray much at all, instead relying on my parents to pull me through and cover me with their prayers.

I originally wrote this book as a poem for an English class assignment in 1988. (Shout out to my English teacher, Mr. Shields.) My mother was so impressed with my poem, she said I should get it published one day.

My godmother, Vashti Yorke, was another very influential prayer warrior in my life as a child. She reminds me so much of Anna from the bible in Luke chapter 2. Her story is very similar; she also lost her husband very early in their marriage. She tells me often that she prays for me each, "morning, noon, and night."

It was my father, though, whom I fondly remember kneeling to pray with me each night at bedtime when I was little. He taught me, "Now I lay me down to sleep," and taught my younger sisters Psalm 23: "The Lord is my shepherd I shall not want." I don't recall exactly how old we were, but it was definitely before I went to kindergarten.

He also had no reservations praying in public when we went out to eat. Back then, when he wanted a good steak, we would head to Ponderosa, and he would pray before having our meal. People would look or stare at him, but it did not matter. My dad would be the one to pray the super-long prayer before meals. The kind of prayer that would have you open one eye to make sure the food was still hot or to sneak a piece of fried plantain because your tummy was rumbling. He would close each meal by praying "In Jesus name we sit at meat. May God now bless the food we eat. Amen" Matthew 9:10 KJV

We had regular family devotions that included singing hymns and praying in our home. This, along with regular church attendance, laid the foundation for who I am today. My parents love to pray, and it is still an vital part of our family routine. Though I still do not pray for an entire hour, even now as an adult, prayer is an essential part of my life.

I pray regularly throughout the day and have my own prayer group (Blessed Trinity—Nicolette, Tanya, and myself), with whom I meet often to pray and study the Bible. I want to create the same atmosphere of prayer in my home for my own family that I had growing up. My daughter has already started her own prayer life. She is too cute! Her prayer is, "Dear God, help me to pray, give you the glory, and do what you say. Please help Mommy and Daddy get me a puppy. In Jesus name, Amen." I'm not sure about that prayer being answered right now. Maybe one day. But she can certainly have her husky pup to play with in this book. My prayer is that this book is inspirational and enjoyed by all who read it.

INTRODUCTION

Prayer is a conversation with God that doesn't have to be super-long or formal. Allow this book to help begin to nurture your prayer life with God. This innate heartfelt desire to pray, love, be kind, and exhibit the character as our Father, God, is the aim of this book. We live in a time where asking for help is a sign of weakness but in actuality the bible encourages us to pray and make our requests known (Philippians 4:6). Our heavenly father hears each and every request for help and welcomes us approaching him in prayer. He created us to be a reflection of him. He is loving and kind; therefore, we should be loving and kind. He is patient, gives comfort and wants us to be like him to each other (Romans 15:5 NKJV).

There is much anxiety, fear, and uncertainty present throughout the world. Many people are trying to find peace and a way to cope during these unprecedented times. For those of us who believe in God, we find peace through prayer and meditation. Reading the Holy Bible is having God speaking directly to our hearts. Applying biblical truths in a practical way is how the believer builds their faith in God. According to biblical principles, instructions on how to live by faith with obedience to God's word positions the believer for success (Joshua 1:8).

There are several ways this book can be effectively utilized. Lord, Teach Me How is three dimensional in that it is a trifecta for application and use. It can be read:

Visually: Each illustration is a meaningful story depicting the poem in a relatable way. The scene is set in Merci-ville, a fictional town in the suburbs of Toronto, Ontario, Canada. The characters are people going through life and how they need help to demonstrate the character of God in everyday situations.

Poetically: Divinely inspired words that rhyme requesting help to attain maturity by building godly characteristics. This is a great way to expose and expand a small child's vocabulary or reflection and introspection as a young teen or adult.

Biblically: For the reader who wants to explore deeper by looking up scriptural references listed below each stanza, the King James Version (KJV) was primarily used as the foundation for this poem. Online resources such as www.Biblegateway.com, with easy-to-read English versions such as the International Children's Bible (ICB) or in different languages are very helpful. Using study Bibles, whether online or paper copy, can bring more clarity.

The reader can choose one, two, or all three applications at any given age or time. There is no right or wrong way or specific time line to reading this book. You can decide to just read the poem and then revisit later and look up scriptures. Some people are visual readers, and that's fine too.

When we see fruit trees, orchards, or vineyards with apples, grapes, melons, all types of fruits, they started from a seed. The growth cycle was not immediate. But then there came roots, soon enough a sprout, then a stem, and then a branch with leaves and buds. Eventually, the long-awaited fruit. In the right environment, there will be growth and a lot of fruit from just one seed. It is the same with building good character. It starts out small, just like a seed, but with the right environment, there will eventually be growth and maturity that is evident when handling or reacting to situations.

The effects of the global pandemic—with restrictions, lockdowns, and the high costs of fuel and food—has many people hostile, bitter, anxious, or depressed. We live in a world where you can hardly find anything or anyone that is reliable these days. From the stock market to friends or family, finding someone you can trust or rely on is getting much harder. The only one who remains faithful is God. You can count on him to always be consistent, never changing, and the same yesterday, presently, and forever. I am willing to be taught by God and ask for help. Join me in this journey to a better version of ourselves.

Proverbs 15:32-33

Good News Translation

[32] If you refuse to learn, you are hurting yourself.
If you accept correction, you will become wiser.

[33] Reverence for the Lord is an education in itself.
You must be humble before you can ever receive honours.

LORD, TEACH ME HOW

Lord, teach me how to pray
For I don't know what to say.
I need to do it every day.
Lord, teach me how to pray.

(Daniel 6:7, 10; Matthew 6:9;
Luke 18:1; 21:36; Colossians 1:3)

Annelize praying with her Husky
pup, Happy, before bedtime.

Lord, teach me how to love.
It's a blessing from above.
It's not good to push or shove.
Lord, teach me how to love.

(Deuteronomy 6:5; John 13:34–35;
Romans 12:10; Ephesians 4:2;
1 Thessalonians 3:12; 1 Peter 1:22; 1 John 4:7)

Tina and Marcus Calum on their wedding day.
They really love each other.

Lord, teach me how to smile
And to go the extra mile.
To be humble as a little child.
Lord, teach me how to smile.

(Proverbs 17:22; Matthew 18:4;
Luke 10:30–37; Colossians 3:23)

Annelize having fun playing with Happy.
He really makes her smile.

Lord, teach me how to share,
To show someone I really care.
This should be my earnest prayer:
Lord, teach me how to share.

(Proverbs 22:9,16; 25:21–22; Isaiah 58:7;
Matthew 25:37–40; Romans 12:13)

Carlos is sharing his lunch with Felipé,
a new hire on construction site.

Lord, teach me how to wait.

My patience is starting to deflate,

And I am in a frenzied state.

Lord, teach me how to wait.

(Psalms 40:1; 69:6; Isaiah 33:2; 40:3; Romans 8:25;

Galatians 5:5; 2 Thessalonians 3:5)

Grandma Millicent is walking very slowly across the street making Tina and Marcus Calum late for their doctor appointment.

Lord, teach me how to sing.
Some happiness that I could bring
To those who do not own a thing.
Lord, teach me how to sing.

(Psalms 96:1; 98:1; Isaiah 42:10; Ephesians 5:19)

Devon singing inspirational music
at an outdoor concert.

Lord, teach me to be meek.

Guide and lead me through the week.

Help me to turn the other cheek.

Lord, teach me to be meek.

(Psalms 37:11; 149:4; Isaiah 61:1; Luke 6:29–31)

Devon helping Grandma Millicent
at the grocery store.

Lord, teach me to be pure.

With your protection, I am sure,

These temptations I'll endure.

Lord, help me to be pure.

(Psalms 18:26; 24:4; 51:10; Matthew 5:8; Titus 1:15)

Annelize wants an after-school snack, but
Mommy said come right home after school.

Lord, help me to be glad
Instead of grumpy, mean, or sad.
To look for the good and not the bad.
Lord, help me to be glad.

(1 Samuel 2:1; Psalms 5:11; 70:4; 118:24;
Habakkuk 3:18; John 16:24; Philippians 4:4)

Friends surprise Tina and Marcus Calum
with gifts at gender reveal party.

Lord, help me be a light.
Not dim or dull, but shining bright,
Your glory seen both day and night.
Lord, help me be a light.

(Psalms 97:11; 112:4; Matthew 5:16;
Ephesians 5:8; 1 John 2:10)

MiLinda giving thanks for her blessings.

Lord, help me to forgive
And not be so defensive,
A longer life that I might live.
Lord, help me to forgive.

(Proverbs 10:12; 17:9; Matthew 6:12-15;
Luke 17:3; Ephesians 4:32)

Felipé lends his brother money many times,
but his brother never pays him back.

Lord, help me not to sin,
A dying soul that I might win,
Those pearly gates to enter in,
Lord, help me not to sin.

(Deuteronomy 6:25; Psalms 1:1–2; 25:4;
Psalm 84:11; 86:11; 119:11; Acts 2:38)

Pastor Feldman hosting an online service
speaking about doing the right thing.

Lord, help me to give praise
For never walking in a daze
Or feeling like I'm in a maze.
Lord, help me to give praise.

(Psalms 33:1; 34:1; 103:1–2;
Psalm 146:1-2; Isaiah 12:4; 1 Peter 1:3)

Tanya just received a promotion at work
with company phone and car.

Lord, help me to be your voice
To all who are hopeless, distressed, or lost,
To make a wise and better choice.
Lord, help me to be your voice.

(Psalms 26:7; 34:2; Acts 15:32;
Romans 12:8; Hebrews 3:13)

Liz speaking at an event encouraging young
people to make right choices.

Lord, teach me all thy will,
Never wordy, just keep still.
My empty heart I know you'll fill.
Lord, teach my all thy will.

(Psalms 46:10; 143:10; John 6:38, 40)

Devon and Liz enjoying a quiet
date night at a café.

Lord, help me to say yes,
That I can stand up to the test.
And then my soul will be so blessed.
Lord, help me to say yes.

(Genesis 22:18; Psalm 26:2; Daniel 3:17–18;
1 Thessalonians 1:9; James 1:12; 1 Peter 1:7)

Grandma Millicent accepting help from
Nicolette crossing the street.

Lord, teach me from thy Word
Obey the things that I have heard,
Increase my faith and stay anchored.
Lord, teach me from thy Word.

(Psalm 119:16, 33, 105; Matthew 4:4;
Romans 10:17; Hebrews 6:19)

Giovanna taking time to read
and study the bible.

Lord, teach me how to trust.
To please God, belief a must.
Confident faith, firm, robust.
Lord, teach me how to trust.

(Psalms 16:1; 18:30; 31:14; 62:8; Romans 1:17;
2 Corinthians 5:7; 1 Timothy 4:10; Hebrews 11:1, 6)

Liz with names of those who trusted
in God; the roll call of faith

So whatever I forgot to ask for,
I pray that you will open the door
To supply each and every need
That in this life I may succeed.
Please teach me what you think is best,
And please, dear Lord, take care of the rest.

Family time walking together
at the park with Happy.

Author Photo Credit: Morgan Kitchen
Freelance Photographer and Creator
Website: www.morgankitchen.com
Instagram: @morgan.xyz

ABOUT THE AUTHOR

Elizabeth Baxter-Lalar grew up in a home where prayer was an important and vital part of her upbringing. "Lord Teach Me How" was penned when the author was 16 years old for an English class poetry assignment. Born and raised in Toronto, Canada to immigrant Jamaican parents, Elizabeth was exposed to the best of both worlds. Going to Jamaica to visit family, eat great food and most importantly get away from the cold Canadian winter is something she enjoys and looks forward to.

Elizabeth is a licensed Registered Pharmacy Technician and has worked in healthcare for over 30 years. As an instructor she taught pharmacy technician students for three years. At work she trained pharmacist and pharmacy technician students orienting them to pharmacy procedures. Her motto is "to be a great teacher, you must be willing to be taught".

Elizabeth can also appreciate that education is not only achieved in the classroom setting but experience can educate in ways that formal education cannot. For many people being "street smart" or having "common sense" is an essential life skill. She is also very mindful of the barriers or limitations that prevent many from completing grade school or attaining post-secondary education which keeps her humble and grateful.

Brought up in the Apostolic/Pentecostal faith, Elizabeth loves attending church services and bible study. "Lord, Teach Me How" is her prayer asking God for help and instruction. Excited to visit new countries, Elizabeth plans to travel and see more of the world. She enjoys writing, reading and helping people embrace learning. Elizabeth is married to Delroy and mother to their daughter Annelize. She currently resides with her family in Toronto, Ontario. To learn more visit her website at: www.lizzybaxter.com

Printed in the United States
by Baker & Taylor Publisher Services